The 100 Most Powerful Prayers for Perfect Customer Service

Toby Peterson

Do You Like Audiobooks?

The experience of having these read to you will, for many people, be more powerful than reading to yourself. For that reason, we are very happy to offer our readers the option to listen to our titles.

If you are not a member of Audible, you can actually get this for free just by signing up. In fact, you can cancel at any time, and keep the book too.

Many of our readers have enjoyed this option. To learn more and get this audiobook for, visit:

PrayerAudiobook.com

Table of Contents

Introduction

In order to attain self-actualization and joy through God, you need to become the designer of your destiny, the author of your life story and the shipwright of your desired vessel. You will need to take responsibility for the success or failure of your life. We know the word responsibility can be somewhat frightening as it not only gives the impression that an enormous amount of work is required but it also speaks to the importance of this task. We agree that taking hold of your life is a significant step which requires a committed mindset. The process, however, this does not necessarily have to be a difficult or massive one. Every process consists of different stages; governing your destiny is certainly no different.

The key is to acknowledge the need to make the adjustments and then begin to make them. Initiating the transformation of your life and well being through prayer is easy. You can start by spending a few short minutes daily in reflection and prayer. Why not take that step of communicating with God, right now? You will be surprised at the powerful effect this simple action will have on your entire life changing process.

The knowledge that God gives you the capabilities to make these changes allows you to emancipate yourself from all fear and doubt. It, therefore, means you will need to first acknowledge that God will provide the mental emotional and spiritual resources needed and then believe in their abilities to accomplish what you need to. The reassurance that God has already given you what you need offers the comfort and security that you are indeed able to successfully make the changes in your life.

The process of regaining the joy, fulfillment, and happiness that God has for your life is effortless with this tried, tested and proven practice. Unlocking your true potential and achieve the goals, dreams, plans and aspirations that God meant for you to have lies with you. That's right, you already have the inherent ability, it simply needs to be accessed and used.

It has been used by the top performers of various groups in society from different industries; finance, education, and even sports. From the financial stalwarts, professors, scholars to Olympic champions, all have used this technique. During this year's Olympic games, it was interesting to find one consistent occurrence with many of the athletes and even more so with the champions. Prior to the signal from the starter for each major race, the competitors close their eyes and pray for a moment. What could they be praying about? Many of these sportsmen and women have won numerous medals and championships prior to the games. They are professionals… shouldn't they have this in the bag? They do, they simply are using the tried, proven and tested technique…

Before commencing they visualize, the event from start to finish with them executing what they have practiced and ultimately winning the said event. These vivid visions are a form of prayer, which has been used for many years. This is one example of how you can tap into the real power of prayer and how God is able to raise you up from the pitfalls any of life's challenges, which weigh you down.

Once you open up yourself to God's positive energy around, the process of creating the outcomes you desire becomes easier. After all, practice makes perfect.

Please do not misunderstand, Prayer isn't intended to make you into an ostrich where you stick your head in the sand and pretend that challenges or negative influences or impacts in your life are non-existent. Instead, prayer encourages you to increase your focus on the progressive end you want and the infinite support that God gives to help you make it happen. Prayer will not mandate that in a day you to get up from your seat and start a profitable multi-billion dollar business out of thin air. *However,* prayer will assist you to find your motivation, own it, and focus on it and in doing so drop all insecurities preventing you from accomplishing your goals. It, therefore, gives you the authority to confidently work with God toward the manifestation of your goals.

Many people lose their ability to focus on the positive energy, which God flows into the world. What with all the overwhelming pressures of daily activities and all the pressures and stresses associated with some, it is almost impossible to keep focus, right? Wrong. Your mindset and attitude will change as you integrate your positive building prayers in your daily routine. You will discover that the more your embrace the positive of any situation, the room for the anxiety and fear which act as stumbling blocks in the lives many people destroying their overall well-being becomes severely decreased.

The prayers here will ensure that you not only determine God's strength to continue your journey towards personal development in spite of the daily challenges and anxieties associated with them. God will release you from the cycle of pessimism and destructive mindset, which has been hindering you from accomplishing your goals for so long.

This book contains a number of prayers designed to help guide and motivate you as you continue on your spiritual journey of change. Any transformation begins in the spiritual realm. Your attitude and mindset determine your reaction to the daily struggles you will encounter. An optimistic attitude and mindset will seek to find the benefit or advantage of every situation; therefore, you will react with less anxiety and stress even when the situation becomes unbearable. These prayers are meant to assist you in maintaining your focus. Please feel free to integrate them into your daily routine. There is no reason to follow a particular routine with the prayers. This may mean you will utilize some while limiting the use of others. Remember the journey life is not unbending it is fluid. Figure out how, when, why and where they work for you. Finally, don't give up at the first attempt, remember everything is a process and practice makes perfect. You will see the difference God has made in your life in the just how your confidence level increases and how your apprehension decreases. The more this happens the closer you are to attaining your goals.

You can use these prayers *for any situation*. Once you start using them, you will find that specific prayers are brought to your consciousness whenever you find yourself in overwhelming situations. This is you learning to replace negative patterns in thinking and responding with prayer. When you notice this happening more frequently, get excited, it means you are growing and the process is working. You are training your mind to work with God's natural flow of energy, which is always positive. We are created to operate as happy, healthy and fulfilled beings. Unfortunately, the complexities of the world have made it more difficult to find and maintain this sweet balance that God has fashioned with us. Damaging thoughts go against God's natural order and will unravel the people who harbor them. Through prayer, you will learn to remain consistent in absorbing and seeking out positive energies. These will transcend into all aspects of your life and influence the people around you. There is no reason to dwell on the loss, defeat, and regrets. It only takes the first few minutes of prayer…lost focus? Regroup and try again. Consider the following as your remedy for results.

1. Review the following list of prayers in full.
2. Pick five (5) to ten (10) prayers that powerfully resonate with you.
3. Repeat several times a day at different intervals. (Minimum five (5) times a day)
4. Use anything available to remind you even on a busy day: a daily planner, phone alarm, etc.
5. Do this consistently for ninety (90) days.

At the end of these ninety (90) days, you will notice, the occurrences in your life are aligned with your expressed desire and no longer just occur by default. You have the results, transfer to the next issue that you wish to change or overcome in your life.

Enjoy!

The 100 Most Powerful Prayers

for Perfect Customer Service

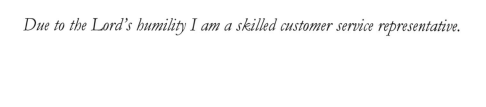

Due to the Lord's humility I am a skilled customer service representative.

I am knowledgeable about the products of our company.

I am a persuasive individual.

I put my customers first.

Thank you Jesus for I am a great communicator.

I am good at convincing other people to buy our products.

I am focused on developing my skills set.

I can deliver a good service to our customers.

I have the product that everyone wants.

Jesus, because of you I instinctively know what my customer needs.

I am in tune with my customer's needs.

I am able to turn any transaction into a beneficial one.

I am becoming a highly skilled customer service representative.

I will exceed my quotas each day.

As a Christian I am a friendly customer service representative.

I have always been a great CSR.

Customer support is one of my natural talents.

I am enthusiastic in everything I do.

I will stay focused on success.

Through Christ I am able to anticipate what my customer needs.

I will be responsive to the needs of my customers.

My success rate will continually increase.

Other people talk about how good I am at helping my customers.

I am destined to be the employee of the month.

Through Jesus' teachings I will continue to grow my customer's

satisfaction rate.

My colleagues see me as one of the best in our company.

Customer service is becoming easier and easier.

I love helping my customers.

I am unfazed by rejection and insults.

I pray to be fierce and resilient.

Customers naturally trust me.

I am respected in this industry.

I can be convincing without being deceitful.

I am equipped to be one of the best CSR in the world.

My customer service career is deeply satisfying all thanks to the Lord.

My customers are important to me.

I start with an incredible level of positive expectation.

I am continually improving and growing.

I am focused on delivering amazing customer service.

Through the holiness of the Lord I take great pleasure in going

out of my way to help my customers.

I am only handed challenges that I am capable of achieving.

I have the ability to listen and have empathy for others.

I will learn the value of hard work.

I will learn to be my best self.

God has granted me to be an effective and powerful customer service representative.

I have the ability to truly understand the needs of others.

I see myself setting records for amazing customer service.

I present solutions that meet our mutual needs and interests.

My honest and positive disposition makes me magnetic and charismatic..

As a child of God I always have the best interest of my clients

and my team in mind.

I am able to constantly improve myself personally and

professionally every day.

I believe in my customer service ability.

I manage my time effectively.

I practice my customer service script every day.

Due to the Lord I am pleasantly persistent with every objection I receive.

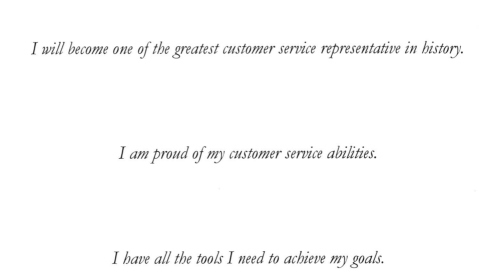

I will become one of the greatest customer service representative in history.

I am proud of my customer service abilities.

I have all the tools I need to achieve my goals.

I attract all the people circumstances and events I need to succeed.

I thank the universe and the Lord for allowing me to be an amazing customer service representative.

I am helping customers with my product.

I am liked by everyone.

I am successful in whatever I do.

I have lots of positive energy flowing through me.

Thank you Jesus because I am given a new opportunity each day.

I learn new customer service ideas each day.

Customer service is fun and easy.

I have the ability to perform better and better.

I have all the leads I need to create the results I want.

Through the grace of God I have a great customer service attitude.

I am receptive and open minded.

I am a person of action.

I effortlessly attract success.

I trust in my abilities to succeed in all I do.

I am a successful customer service representative all thanks to the Lord.

I am smart and wise.

I create amazing business opportunities.

I make customer service look very easy.

I love my job.

I am passionate in rendering service to my customers with god by my side.

I am a perfect match for customer service.

I am an achiever.

I am extremely grateful for the chance to be of service to others.

I am terrific at what I love doing.

Because I am with God I will meet amazing people through amazing customer service.

I have a high degree of personal integrity.

I will put out extra effort.

I will emphasize the positive in everything I do.

I look at the good that can come out of every situation.

I am organized because I plan my days and follow my plans with the guidance of the Lord.

I do the most productive things at every given moment.

I am able to enthusiastically support my co-workers.

I am able to deliver superior customer service to my clients.

I can communicate clearly and powerfully.

Through great faith I am in great shape and fantastic health.

I am a good listener.

I sincerely care about the needs of my customers.

I have positive personal power that is contagious.

I am intelligent and innovative about all that I do.

By God's grace I generate perfect customer service and positive results.

The 100 Most Powerful Prayers

for Instant Persuasion

Jesus, because of you I am a persuasive person with a great personality.

I can get people to listen to what I have to say.

I can persuade people to do my bidding.

I will use my persuasion to lift other up.

I pray my persuasion is pure, good, and strong.

I am a great speaker with persuasive qualities.

I will persuade others to do good things.

I am influential, and I am very persuasive.

I can persuade even the most stubborn people.

God almighty, please help me persuade even strangers to do well.

I will use my persuasion to change the world.

I will use persuasion to make people happy.

The world is better off with my persuasion.

I am good at teaching other people with persuasion.

Thank you Jesus for people who want to hear what I have to say.

I can bend even the most negative ear.

I will make people smile with my words.

I will persuade others to believe in themselves.

I will persuade myself to believe in me.

Through the Lord's Holiness I can persuade others to lend a

helping hand.

I can persuade others to be my friend.

Persuasion is a skill that I love having.

I will use my skill for good only.

I will never use persuasion for any negativity.

By God's grace I can persuade a rock to do my bidding.

I will continue to work on my persuasion skills.

I am great at what I do, and I love it.

I love myself and my amazing skills.

Persuasion is a powerful tool if used right.

Through Jesus Christ I will do what I can to persuade the world.

I will use persuasion to bring positivity.

Persuading others is a big part of who I am.

I have great skills, and I use them well.

I will hone my skills to near perfection.

God has granted me when I speak, others tend to listen to me.

I am charismatic, and that draws people to me.

My smile helps people trust me easier.

I am great at what I do and love every minute.

I will use my persuasion to help strangers.

Through the guidance of our Lord I will use my persuasion to help friends.

I will never use persuasion to hurt others.

I am a moral person and use persuasion for good.

Persuading others is a part of who I am.

I find conversing with others to be an easy task.

Through the grace of God I am a great conversationalist with strangers.

I do not have to buy people to get things done.

I can persuade people who have no motivation.

I will use persuasion to motivate others.

I will lead others with my persuasion.

Jesus please guide me to use my persuasion to be a good role model.

I am a good person, and I enjoy my talent.

There is nothing wrong with using persuasion.

I am a influential person, and I work with that.

I learn more from other persuasive people.

As a Christian I enjoy meeting others and learning new things.

There is much this world has left to teach me.

There is much I have left to teach others.

I use persuasion to open people's eyes.

I am always on the lookout for new friends.

Because I am with God, I will never persuade others to steal.

I will never persuade others to cheat.

I will never persuade people to hurt others.

I will never use persuasion for evil.

I will only use persuasion for good.

Due to the Lord, I persuade other people to the best of my ability.

I can use my abilities to change the world.

I can teach others to also change the world.

People need motivation, I persuade them to find it.

I am doing a lot of good with my talent.

Through the guidance of our Lord I help a lot of people with my talent.

I can persuade people to help themselves.

I have a lot to give to the world.

This world has a lot to teach me.

I feel that I am great with persuasion.

Through Jesus' teachings, I am able to be strong in my abilities.

Persuasion is for good only.

If I have used it wrong, I will fix that today.

Mistakes happen, I will learn from them.

I will speak to others as I like to be spoken to.

God please help me to understand that part of persuading is listening.

I am a great listener, and a great friend.

People want to listen to me because I care.

I do not force others to listen.

I am okay when people don't want to listen.

Through the Lord's Holiness persuasion is good for anyone

who needs help.

I can persuade others to change their lives for good.

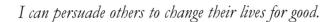

I will help an addict through persuasion.

I can help a convict through persuasion.

The suggestive mind is my playground.

God has granted me my abilities to help the homeless.

I can use my abilities to help the rich.

I can help anyone who needs my help.

I can help people help themselves.

I can persuade people to lean on me.

With God by my side I can be a rock for those who need it.

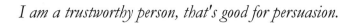

I am a trustworthy person, that's good for persuasion.

I will not break another's trust.

I will not break my own trust.

I have a code to live by.

Through great faith I love being a persuasive person, it is a part of me.

The 100 Most Powerful Prayers

for Money

Because I am with God, I will have more money than I ever

dreamed possible.

I deserve money in my life.

I have great wealth flowing into my life all the time.

I always have all the money that I want and need.

Through great faith, I am becoming wealthier with each day that passes

I derive my wealth from my own greatness.

I attract abundance in all aspects of my life.

I am prosperous and living in abundance.

I am enriching my life by increasing my income.

I am never far from my next financial opportunity with God by my side.

I easily see opportunities to make money.

I have unlimited success and prosperity.

I want for nothing in my life.

I make money come to me with little effort.

Due to Lord's humility, I am able to find prosperity in each endeavor I embark on.

I seize new opportunities to make money each day.

I will make more money easily and effortlessly.

I will have a limitless abundance of wealth.

I am successful in each of my business ventures.

God has granted me to meet all of my financial needs instantaneously.

I have the power to be successful.

I am naturally magnetized to wealth and prosperity.

I have a life filled with wealth and abundance.

I am now starting to accumulate large amounts of money.

I am locked on the path to wealth and success with Jesus' mercy.

I am surrounded by prosperity and greatness.

I am endlessly and extremely successful.

I expect the best in life and I am getting it now.

I am able to live the life of my dreams.

As a Christian I have the power within myself to create wealth.

I enjoy a life overflowing with abundant wealth.

I have unlimited ability to achieve and make money.

I make money with every move I make.

I am enjoying multiple streams of income.

Through Jesus Christ, I am living a rich and happy life.

I have an endless well of incredible ideas to make money.

I see wealth building opportunities everywhere.

I always get the things that I desire in life.

I choose to live a life of abundance and prosperity.

I am not limited in the amount of money I can make because

of the Lord.

I am increasing my net worth every day.

I am a powerful magnet for prosperity.

I find unexpected income in every place I look.

I deserve to live a wealthy life full of the best things.

Through God almighty, I always have enough money for the

life I want to live.

I am led by the universe to all the wealth I need.

I am naturally a wealthy and successful person.

I have an amazing ability to attract wealth into my life.

I make the wealth that I seek come to me.

Jesus Christ, I will always be wealthy and prosperous for my entire life.

I have an endless and immediate supply of money.

I live a life free of debt and financial stress.

I am able to create wealth with any resources that surround me.

I have endless money making ideas.

I have more money than I could ever dream of spending because of my

unwavering faith in the Lord.

I receive wealth from many sources in my life.

I am happy and grateful to be wealthy.

I will always have more than I need.

I easily accumulate and share my wealth.

I am proud to be happy, healthy, and wealthy all thanks to the Lord.

I use my wealth to make the world a better place.

I welcome a lifestyle of wealth with open arms.

I am successful because I know what I want and I get it.

I have easy access to an abundance of the things I desire.

Due to the Lord's grace, I am proud of the wealth that

I have gained.

I am open and receptive to all the riches the universe offers me.

I constantly discover new avenues of generating income.

I use my wealth to enrich the lives of those around me.

I take actions that create a constant stream of prosperity.

I am in tune with the abundant giving energy of the universe, thank you Jesus.

I am the master of my own financial well-being.

I often find that money unexpectedly comes into my life..

I have more money coming to me constantly.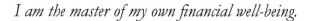

I am naturally attuned to the energy of prosperity.

Through God I turn each new situation into a business opportunity.

I enjoy all of the freedom that money brings into my life.

I have more than enough money to share with the world around me.

I am able to have all the money I want.

I am inherently attracting a stream of money toward my life.

As a child of Christ, I will not ever have to struggle financially again.

I instinctively walk the path to greater wealth.

I want for nothing that my wealth cannot provide.

I become more valuable each day that passes.

I can use even the most meager resources to generate money.

I have total control of how much money I can make with the

Lord's guidance.

I find opportunities to generate new income in unexpected places.

I have an ability to gain wealth that knows no limits.

I have no interruption in my flow of income.

I need very little to work with to start generating money.

By God's grace, I make the choice to live a prosperous and abundant life.

I draw upon a personal well of unlimited wealth generating energy.

I make large amounts of money without even trying.

I am in complete control of my growing finances.

I lead a happy and wealthy life.

I am never worried about where my money will come from because

I believe in God.

I know how and when to spend and save money.

I fearlessly dive into new business ventures.

I am an amazing businessperson.

I negotiate every business deal to my great advantage.

Due to the Lord, I will never be out of money ever again.

The 100 Most Powerful Prayers

for Anxiety

O Lord, I know anxiety is a thing of the past, please help

me conquer it.

I feel exactly how I choose to feel with God's help.

Almighty Father, please let me be in a healthy and exciting

place in my life.

Thank you for making me feel extremely confident and in

control, O God.

Heavenly Father, please make me feel less anxious every day.

Lord, thank you for making me focus only on what makes me feel good.

I eat healthy & exercise everyday with God's blessings,

because it strengthens my mind.

Lovingly Lord, please let me practice sleep hygiene because

it sets the tone for my next day.

Thank you for making me incredibly strong, O God.

Through Christ's will, I am most disciplined when it

comes to choosing how I feel.

God, please make me believe in myself and have full control

over my choices.

Lord, help me choose to feel good about myself.

I choose everyday to use prayer and get results with God's guidance.

Almighty God, please let me challenge myself to get out of

my comfort zone.

Thank you for making me feel powerful in my own body, O' Lord.

I love doing things that make me feel good with Christ's assistance.

Dear Father, please help me seek greater opportunities

outside of my comfort zone.

Almighty God, please help me write down my challenging

goals to expand my horizon.

My Lord, please let me control anxiety so it would become

a thing of the past.

I used to have anxiety, now I am full of confidence with God's grace.

Please make me stay calm, cool and collected, O Lord.

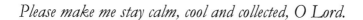

Lovingly God, thank you for making me at peace with my mind.

Lovingly God, thank you for making me at peace with my body.

I am so grateful for my bravery and composure to you, O. Lord.

Christ, please make me remain calm when things don't go as planned.

My God, I humbly ask you to guide me in choosing to feel

good and making healthy lifestyle choices.

I hold all responsibility for my life, O Lord, and I always

need your direction.

I am content with my life through Christ's blessing.

I love myself as much as I love the Creator.

Please help me to decide how I feel in all circumstances, my Lord.

God, please guide me in keeping healthy relationships only in my life.

Almighty Father, please help me choose the path in life.

Dear Lord, please guide my confidence in all environments.

I visualize bravery in all aspects I require it in Christ's favour.

I had panic, but that was in the distant past. Through

Christ, I am now calm.

Dear God, please keep me protected and at peace in public and private.

Lord, thank you for making me feel safe.

Heavenly Father, I humbly ask you to make me confront anxiety, and feel it fade away quickly.

I feel like I can conquer the world through God's blessing.

My God, please guide me to focus on my strengths.

Dear Lord, please help me maintain a posture that exudes

confidence & strength.

Almighty Christ, please guide me to stay hydrated & eat

nutritious food for my mind.

O Lord, I humbly ask you to give me the wisdom to

exercise daily to stimulate my body and mind.

I am a champion through God's guidance.

God, I give thanks for my life to you.

I am praying to the Lord to grow more and more confident every day.

My God, thank you for letting me help others & stop worrying about myself every day.

Please help me get relaxed in every part of my body, O' Lord.

Thank you, Father, for letting me look forward to my amazing life to come.

I am anxiety-free because of the Lord.

I love being in social situations with the Almighty's grace.

Heavenly God, please guide me to ask questions about others & not worry about myself always.

I love myself today and everyday just as I love the Lord above.

I take deep conscious breaths throughout each day with God's spirit surrounding me.

Dear Lord, please help me to replace negative thoughts with positive thoughts.

I am so grateful to the Creator above for everything I

already have in my life.

I feel secure and safe in God's arms.

Thank you, Lord, for providing me positive energy in my life.

Almighty God, please let me have thoughts of confidence in

all situations.

I inhale calmness with each breath you give me, O' Lord.

Dear God, please make me feel freedom and make me worry-free.

With the Lord's guidance, I love being with people because

it brings out the best in me.

Thank you, Almighty God for giving me room for peace

and prosperity in my life.

Lord, please guide me to train my mind everyday.

I embrace opportunity to speak in public with God's blessing.

My Lord, I humbly ask you to guide me to let go of all

worries in my life.

O God, I need your presence for me to be comfortable in

group settings.

I will enjoy the present moment through the Lord's will.

I am blessed with an incredible life by the Creator above.

Thank you, Almighty Father for making me an optimistic

person & great things continue to happen to me.

Dear God, please make me more comfortable than I used to

be in social situations.

I appreciate those around me, O' Lord.

My Lord, please help me surround myself with people I

want to be like.

I remove doubt from my mind for what I want to achieve

with your guidance, O' God.

Thank you for providing me more confidence day by day, Dear God

Almighty Father, I am grateful for you blessing me with

energy and enthusiasm.

I feel naturally at peace through God's grace.

O God, please guide me in having full control over my emotions.

Heavenly Father, please make me courageous when it is needed.

With God's guidance, I must fail to succeed & I am

comfortable with that.

Lord, please help me figure it out.

Dear Father, please guide me on meeting new people.

Thank you, Lord, for blessing me incredibly high self-esteem.

I am getting better in group & public settings all the time;

thanks all to You, O Lord.

I can fully relax when I'm in public with God's grace.

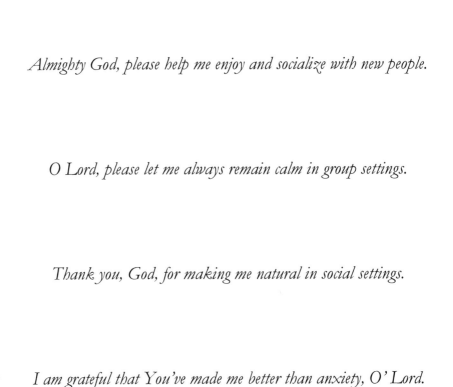

Almighty God, please help me enjoy and socialize with new people.

O Lord, please let me always remain calm in group settings.

Thank you, God, for making me natural in social settings.

I am grateful that You've made me better than anxiety, O' Lord.

I know exactly how to relax through Christ's guidance.

Thank you for always making me feel calm, Almighty Father.

I fully trust myself as I trust in You, O' God.

Dear Lord, thank you for giving me incredible inner strength.

I remain true to myself as I remain to You, O Lord.

Heavenly Father, please help me to attract positive individuals

into my life.

Dear God, please help me to choose what I want to think

about in all situations.

I control my life and I need You to guide me, my Lord.

O Lord, please guide me to replace any feeling I choose.

Thank you, Lovingly Father, because I am able to maintain

focus whenever needed.

Anxiety is a thing of the past because of your help, O' God.

The 100 Most Powerful Prayers

for Becoming Alpha Male

Jesus, because of you I am a dominant man, and it shows.

I will not cower to other people.

I am understanding, yet firm.

I am strong and seductive.

Because I am with God, I am calm and relaxed.

I show dominance always.

I ooze confidence when I walk.

I breath in strength and power.

I am not cruel, just intense.

I pray I will transform into the man I am meant to be.

No one will take power from me.

I will protect my loved ones

I will protect myself.

No one will bring harm to those around me.

Because I am with God, it is my duty to be strong.

It is my duty to be just.

I am a natural leader of others.

Women are attracted to me.

I attract other people when I walk in a room.

Due to the Lord, others trust me without reason.

I will be an alpha male.

My confidence in myself is solid.

My confidence in my abilities is strong.

I can take on any obstacle with pride.

Jesus please guide me to not fall to a weaker male.

I will not fall to other's temptations.

An alpha must lead, and lead I shall.

I will make a great alpha male.

I will love and protect my partner.

Through Christ I am a great man to be alpha.

Being alpha runs in my veins.

I am a natural born leader.

Other people follow me when I lead.

I have influential power and persuasion.

God almighty, please help me use my strength to protect others.

I am an alpha male.

I visualize myself being empowered.

I may not be there yet, but I will be soon.

I have the mind of an alpha.

God has granted me the body of an alpha.

I have the spirit of an alpha.

I will be the best alpha male around.

I am an empowered male figure.

I will encourage others as well.

Through the guidance of our Lord an alpha protects his pack, I shall

protect mine.

I will support those around me.

I will not take my status for granted.

I become more assertive each day.

I take what I want with power.

As a Christian I am also very caring.

Women lean on me for decisions.

I attract women a lot easier now.

I can find my love as alpha.

I can love myself as alpha.

Through Jesus' teachings, I am confident in my abilities as a man.

I am confident that I can perform well.

Being alpha will not corrupt me.

I will not use power for evil.

I will be a moral alpha.

Through our Lord I will take care of those around me.

I will be confident in my own abilities.

I will depend on no one for my happiness.

I am strong, independent, and a great alpha.

No one will undermine my authority.

Because I am with God, I will command attention in a room.

I will be a good person throughout.

Being alpha will not change me.

Being alpha will enhance my good qualities.

I am a better person with confidence.

Through the grace of God I will handle all things with care.

I will handle all things with strength.

I have a good head on my shoulders.

I am smart enough to be an alpha.

I will not stand for any challengers.

God almighty, please help me not stand for negativity.

I will be a positive leader.

I will be a positive person.

Being alpha does not mean being mean.

I will be a kind leader to all.

Through Jesus' teachings, other people can depend on me.

I do not need to depend on others.

I am a swift person.

I have a sharp mind.

I can handle any situation with ease.

Jesus, because of you confidence flows through me.

I will speak with an authoritative tone.

When I speak, others will listen.

I will no longer hide in a crowd.

I will be notices when I enter a room.

By God's grace men will want to be me.

Women will want to be with me.

I will appreciate myself more.

I appreciate myself now.

I can do anything as an alpha male.

Due to the Lord, I trust myself to make the right choices.

Others trust me to make the right choices.

I will help others with my strength.

I will help others with my voice.

I will help others with my influence.

Through our Lord I choose to be a strong and influential alpha male today.

Thank You!

I want to sincerely thank you for reading this book!

Let me finish though by saying the work isn't done here. These must be put to use repetitively, and on a daily basis to see changes in your life.

Remember to follow the ninety-day plan outlined in the introduction to maximize your results.

Can I ask you for a very quick favor? Can you leave a review on our Amazon.com detail page to tell us about your progress and how you enjoyed the book?
amazon.com/review/create-review

We take the time to go over each review personally, and your feedback in invaluable to us as writers, and others that wish to see the same change in their lives as you:)

Thank You!

CONSCIOUS
VISUALIZATION

5 Simple Steps To
Condition Your Mind to
Create The Life of Your
Dreams...

JASON THOMAS
foreword by TOBY PETERSON

Table of Contents

Foreword

Until recent times, mostly sports psychologists and personal trainers that were teaching athletes to visualize success valued visualization. After much studying and application, however, it has been found that the power of conscious visualization can help people from all walks of life reach their goals.

Do some research yourself. You will find athletes, movie actors, entrepreneurs, and people from all areas and occupations that have learned the incredible power of visualization and how it can help them succeed in achieving their wildest dreams. Conscious visualization propels you past the obstacles that you may face and helps you reach the biggest goals that you set for yourself.

Now, get out there and be the best version of you that you can be. This book is going to teach you all of the visualization techniques that you need so that you soar over your obstacles and achieve even the most challenging of goals that you set for yourself.

I want to wish you luck and success as you start, continue on, and complete your journey.

Toby Peterson

Introduction

Oprah Winfrey, Will Smith, and Arnold Schwarzenegger are just three of many well-known celebrities that have attributed at least some of their success to the power of conscious visualization. There are stories from celebrities around the world that prove one thing; visualization can be the driving factor in your success.

It is no surprise that these and many other successful individuals rely on visualization to power them forward. Stop for a moment and think about the last time you were faced with an intimidating situation, whether it was a presentation at work or meeting your future in-laws for the first time. How did you feel beforehand? What thoughts were running through your head?

If you are like most people who have not yet learned the power of conscious visualization, then you were probably worried about the situation you were faced with. You may have even made yourself panic over the situation, by worrying about what could go wrong instead of what could go right.

The key to conscious visualization is that it helps you overcome obstacles. When you can visualize the end result, you can power yourself through any of the roadblocks in your way and give yourself a confidence in yourself that you did not even know you had.

The good news is that while many successful people attribute their success to conscious visualization, you can do it too. You do not have to be wealthy or extraordinarily talented to make your splash in the world and reach your goals. The only thing that you need is the power of your own mind and the steps included in this book.

As you read, you will find that your results may improve by listening to the visualizations instead of just reading them. If this is the case, you can purchase the audio version of this book.

In this book, you will find five separate steps that will propel you to your own success. You will also find a bonus chapter, which addresses affirmations that you can use to further the success of conscious visualization and boost your confidence in yourself. Once you have reached the end of this book, you will have learned a regimen that will propel you forward to reach your greatest dreams. You will be able to overcome obstacles, feel confident in yourself, and so much more. All you have to do is visualize- read on to find out how.

Chapter 1 - Step 1 - Setting Your Goals

The first step of conscious visualization is knowing what your goals are. In order for visualization to propel you to success, you must be able to pinpoint the things that you want in life. From there, you must be able to choose a realistic and directed visualization that is going to help you reach success. This chapter will teach you all about setting goals and the techniques that you can use to keep them in the forefront of your mind.

How to Properly Set Goals

Be Realistic and Have a Plan for Follow Through

Consider for a moment that your goal is to be rich one day. You start every morning by visualizing yourself sitting in a bathtub of money. How likely do you think it is that this will work?

The truth is that whether or not the visualization works depends on your course of action following the visualization. Imagine one scenario where the person visualizing wealth does not have a job. They live at their parent's house, do not put in job applications or make wise investments, and do nothing to better themselves. Even with a great visualization, it is very unlikely that this person is going to reach their goals.

Imagine a second scenario. This person also dreams of great riches and their visions are perfect down to the satisfaction. When they go to spend money on something they don't need, they may think of this vision. Instead of spending the money, they invest it in a savings account that accrues interest and increases their wealth over time. This person accompanied their visualizations with the right actions.

As you are setting your goal, it is important to have a plan of action as well. You can visualize success all you want, but it will not work if you are intentionally sabotaging yourself or hiding in your parent's basement all day. You have to have the follow through of the right actions in order to reach your goals.

Be Specific

One of the keys to successful visualization is being specific. In order for your visualizations to be successful, you must make your goals as successful as possible. For example, do not imagine yourself becoming wealthy. Instead, imagine yourself being wealthy by doing well in the stock market, opening the business you always dreamed of, being promoted in your place of work, or cashing in on wise investments one day.

Break Your Goal Into Steps

If you have a long-term goal, you will find that it is helpful to break it up into steps. Every goal that you have is a process, especially in the long-term. You will not just rise to the top in your company from a lower level position. Instead, you will go through a series of promotions until you are at the top. As you are planning each goal, take a moment to break it down into a series of steps. If you want a car, for example, you may set goals to save a certain amount of money back each month until you can afford it.

Write Your Major Goals Down on Note Cards

If you have several goals, then you may find it beneficial to write each individual goal down on note cards. On the front, you can write down a summary of the goal. On the back, break your goal down into steps. You may also find it helpful to write down helpful affirmations that pertain to that specific goal or your specific visualization that you use to picture the goal. If applicable, you can also write down the timeframe in which you want to complete each step of the goal.

Chapter 2 - Step 2 - Daily Visualization of Your Goals

In order for visualization to be successful, it is important to make it part of a daily regimen. During this regimen, you will be visualizing success of all of your objectives for the day and tie them back to your larger goals. As you are reading about the regimen in the conclusion of this book, you should refer back to this chapter for instructions.

The Science of Conscious Visualization

When you carry out an activity or a thought, a certain set of neurons lights up, as well as the neural pathways between them. Conscious visualization works because visualizing a certain scenario lights up the neural pathways that tell the brain to perform that action, whatever it may be. Every time that you carry out this activity, the neural pathways strengthen and the mind will eventually be able to carry out the task instantaneously. Visualizing certain scenarios frequently, therefore, strengthens the neural pathways and makes these behaviors easier. This means you will be more likely to perform well when you are actually doing the activity or behavior.

For more evidence and information on the way that visualization works, check out the references section at the end of the book.

Planning Your Objectives

As you will learn later in this book, there is more than one type of conscious visualization that can help you on the road to success. For this type of visualization, you will want to start by planning out your objectives for the day. Make a physical list of the things that you want to accomplish. These can be tasks like making time for yourself or working on housework or they can be behavioral changes like being more confident or interacting more with your coworkers.

Visualizing Your Objectives

Go to a quiet area where you can be comfortable and relax. Sit or lie down and relax in silence for a few moments. Then, read over your list of objectives to get them fresh in your mind. Visualize yourself going through your day and completing each of these objectives. Feel yourself confidently tacking each item on your list and physical sensations that you may experience. Give yourself confidence that you will be able to complete each of your goals by envisioning each of them.

As you visualize, you may find it helpful to observe yourself in first person. As you go through your vision, pay close attention the way everything feels. Imagine yourself from the inside of your body and that you are interacting with people and your surroundings.

Visualizing Your Success

Imagine yourself basking for a moment after each small success, thinking about how the task accomplished a goal (a clean house can reduce stress) or how it will help propel you forward in life. Visualize yourself completing all of your goals and how it will feel when you are rewarding yourself at the end of the day.

Example of Daily Conscious Visualization

For the purpose of this exercise, imagine that you have a note card with the following goals written down on it:

> To reach out to your coworkers by inviting someone to have lunch with you
>
> To make it to the gym after work
>
> To start your research for a presentation at work
>
> To spend at least an hour not working and having 'me' time before bed

Sit or lie down in your quiet space. Close your eyes and take a few deep breaths to relax. Then, read the goals that you have written on the note card to bring them to the forefront of your mind. Alternatively, you can visualize each goal separately and read the objectives on the note card one at a time.

Start by visualizing yourself walking through the doors to your job. Feel your confidence as you walk toward one of your coworkers and ask them to lunch. Visualize them accepting your invitation. Then, imagine conversing with them over lunch, being as specific as you can. Imagine the happiness that you will feel at the chance to make a new friend and the sense of companionship that you feel from interacting with others.

Then, visualize yourself leaving from work and feeling energized. You eat a small snack and drive (or walk) to the gym. You have a satisfying workout. When you finish, imagine the sense of accomplishment and pride that you feel for doing something for yourself and working toward your weight loss goals.

Next, imagine yourself driving to your house. You cook and eat dinner. Once you are finished, you walk to the computer and begin your research for work. Visualize the keyboard beneath your fingers as you take notes. After you are satisfied with the work that you have done, visualize yourself pausing to bask in your sense of accomplishment. Enjoy the relief that you feel with the project now being started.

Finally, imagine what you are going to do before bedtime. Now that you are satisfied with your work for the night, you do not go straight to bed and watch television or play on your phone until you pass out. Think about what you want to do for yourself, whether you want to read a book, take a hot bath, do yoga, color, or do another activity. Imagine the activity from start to finish and then feel the sense of pride that fills you after completing all of your objectives for the day. Focus on this feeling until it gives you a warm, glowing feeling of happiness and success.

Chapter 3 - Step 3 - Learning to Relax in Stressful Situations

While this book is about creating a regular regimen for success, you will find there are times where conscious visualization can help you relax to handle a stressful situation better. Some situations where this technique may be applicable include before a job interview, test, presentation at school or work, a first date, meeting your spouse's parents, or talking to someone in an uncomfortable situation. Visualization can often be used for these types of encounters on a per-case basis to help you come out successful on the other side.

Identifying Your Challenge Situations

In order to know when visualization can benefit you throughout the day, you must be able to identify which situations call for a little extra help. Some people, for example, fear public speaking and may struggle any time that they must speak to a group. Others may find that their most challenging situations include encounters with others.

A good way to identify which situations stress you is to pay attention to physical cues and your thought patterns. Some physical cues that you may experience in a stressful situation include excessive sweating, clammy palms, and a rapid heartbeat. Some common thought patterns include self-defeating thoughts like "I can't do this," "I'm going to do terrible," and "I'm not good enough," as well as worries about what may go wrong in the situation.

If you find yourself struggling to notice specific patterns, consider keeping a journal. Make note of any of the times that you feel overly stressed or notice the thoughts and feelings from the previous paragraph. Write down the time of day, what was happening at the time, and which thoughts or physical sensations you experienced. You should also make note of who was around at the time, what you were thinking about, and any other relevant information. If you keep good notes, you will eventually be able to go over them and recognize the various patterns. Once you see the patterns, you will be able to plan for stressful situations before they even occur.

Visualization for Challenging Situations

Go To a Quiet Room

Before you tackle the challenging situation, put yourself in a calm, quiet environment where you can focus. If you are at home, this could be your bedroom, your garden, or another area you have set up. If you are at work, a good place to relax could be an empty conference room or your office. Sit or lie down and close your eyes. Pay close attention to your breathing and bring yourself into a state of relaxation.

Picture Your Success

Once you are relaxed, picture your success overcoming the obstacle from the second that you walk through the door. Be as detailed as you can and visualize yourself overcoming every obstacle that comes in your way. Here is an example of a visualization that you could use if you were giving a presentation at work:

You are standing outside of the office door, knowing that you are about to walk in and give a presentation to a room full of people. You are dressed nicely, well groomed, and feeling confident. You turn the doorknob and walk confidently across the room to the front with your head held high. Your presentation is already set up, including any visuals or power point material that you may have. You casually introduce yourself to the group and give a brief summary of what is about to be discussed. Then, you pull note cards out of your pocket and begin to give your presentation, only glancing at the note cards to keep you on track. Your voice is calm and sure.

At the end of the presentation, some of your audience has questions. You are well prepared and feel confident as you are answering their questions. At the end of the presentation, you feel pleased and know that the committee values your idea.

Take a Few Breaths and Succeed

After you have done your visualization, you are ready to tackle your challenge. Take a few deep breaths, imagine the feeling of success once again, and excel in the stressful situation.

Chapter 4 - Step 4 - Using Visualization to Boost Your Self-Confidence

One of the reasons that visualization works is because it increases your self-confidence. Think about the last time you faced a situation that you worried about. Did you panic yourself into thinking all of the bad things that could happen? What was the result of the situation? If you did fret over what could go wrong instead of what could go right, it is likely that you set yourself up for failure. After all, how can you be confident about the outcome of a situation when you have so many doubts about it in the first place? In this chapter, you will learn how to use visualization to boost your self-confidence so that you stop doubting yourself in challenging situations.

#1: Identify Why You Are Lacking Self-Confidence

Before you can go about changing your lack of self-confidence, you must understand the reasons that you act and think the way that you do. Below are some of the most common reasons that people lack self-confidence.

You Talk Negatively to Yourself

Have you ever heard the expression, "I am my own self critic."? While being a critic of yourself can help you find your flaws to improve them, it is not helpful if you are holding yourself back with your criticisms. For example, people who talk negatively to themselves often set themselves up for failure before they are even faced with a situation. They may have to give a presentation at work and talk down to themselves beforehand, saying things like "I am not good enough," "They will not like my idea," or "Why should I even bother?" The problem with this is that talking negatively to yourself makes you think that you will fail. If you believe that you are going to fail, it is much more likely that you will have a bad outcome.

You Are Afraid to Take Risks

Some people just find themselves more outgoing than others. Some people believe that this is a personality difference that is ingrained from birth, while others blame it on a child's upbringing. Regardless, if you find that you are afraid of taking risks, it becomes more likely that you will lack self-confidence. The reason for this is that you probably had fewer experiences because you are more likely to say "no" to trying new things. This lack of experience can result in a lack of self-confidence.

You Do Not Know How to Be Confident

Have you ever found yourself looking at a friend or coworker and wondering how they are able to be so confident? It seems that some people are born confident, while others struggle even to interact with other people on a day-to-day basis. If you find yourself feeling as if confidence is something that you are born with and that you did not get the gene, remember that it is a learned skill. Anyone can be confident in his or her abilities- it just takes the right self-talk and visualizations to encourage you on your way.

#2: Know How Confident People Act

The first step in uncovering your own confidence is knowing how confident people act. Make a list of behaviors of confident people. For example, to you, confidence may mean talking to people more, making your ideas known, being able to showcase your talents, or not being afraid to bring up difficult subjects. Think about the way that confident people walk, how they interact with others, and how they make their ideas known. If you do not know, spend some time watching some of the most confident people you know.

#3: Change Your Thoughts and Behaviours

Once you know how confident people behave, you can start to act that way. You will find that everything you do can exude confidence if you do it properly. The way you walk, talk, and interact with others can have profound effects on the level of confidence that you feel. Once you know how confident people act, start to follow in their footsteps to develop your own self-confidence.

If you find yourself struggling with negative thinking that is costing you your self-confidence, it can be important to change the way that you think. Start by recognizing your negative thought patterns (I am worthless, I cannot do this, I will mess this up) and changing them by stating the opposite. Build yourself up instead of tearing yourself down and you will find that the result is greater confidence.

#4: Visualize Yourself Confidently Handling Your Challenges

Once you are ready to make the commitment to self-confidence, use visualization to see yourself feeling confident in everything that you do. When you are doing your daily visualizations, feel the way that your shoulders and back stretch out when you stand tall and envision yourself speaking clearly and loudly. Imagine the warmth that feels your chest when you are confident enough in your ideas that you can freely share them with others and the friendships that may result from being more outgoing and communicating with others. Clearly visualize yourself tackling each challenge and then feel the satisfaction when you do so.

Example of Visualization for Self-Confidence

In this scenario, you have been gabbing with a coworker for several weeks. You decide to ask him/her out on a date but you are incredibly nervous. Before you talk to your coworker, you would perform this visualization.

The morning before, you carefully pick out one of your favorite outfits that is attractive and comfortable. You remember to put on deodorant and brush your teeth and your clothes are nice. When you get to the office, you visualize yourself entering the door with your head up and your shoulders back, exuding an air of confidence. You walk to the water cooler and take a deep breath. Your words come out clear, "Will you go to lunch with me?" Visualize that your coworker has said yes and imagine the sense of excitement and content that you will feel once you have asked.

Chapter 5 - Step 5 - Overcoming Obstacles

Conscious visualization is all about visualizing success and only thinking of the positive things that will happen in your life, right? Well, yes and no. Positive visualization can help propel you to success. However, you do have to realize that not everything that happens in life is in your control. Additionally, it is natural for you to face obstacles or have things come up that challenge your goals and your motivation toward them, as well as your peace of mind. This chapter will teach you about the techniques that you can use to overcome your obstacles so that they do not get in the way of your positive visualization.

Let Go of Things That Are Out of Your Control

It would be very unnatural for someone to go through life without any types of struggle. Even if you use visualization to fill your life with as much positivity, self-confidence, and success that you can muster, things are going to arise that may set you back. For example, you may have fitness goals but then have a relative you were close to pass away. There may be a few days where you struggle to make it to the gym. In this case, it is best to remember that you cannot control what has happened. Allow yourself time to grieve and forgive yourself if you skip the gym for a few days. What matters is that you will get back on track, regardless of the setbacks you experience.

Visualization Example for Releasing Negative Thoughts

For this exercise, go to a quiet area where you can relax. Sit or lie in a comfortable position and start to breathe. As you breathe, focus your mind on all of your worries and negative thoughts. Allow yourself to dwell for one breath cycle. Then, inhale a deep breath through your nose, filling your stomach and chest until you cannot any longer. Imagine that this breath is all of the negativity inside of you. Exhale it in a slow but strong woosh, breathing out through your mouth.

Repeat this visualization a few times. Then, start to breathe in more slowly and deliberately. Visualize that positive vibes and feelings are filling you with each inward breath. If you find yourself dwelling on any more negative thoughts, exhale them out. Do this until nothing but positivity exists inside of you.

Look At Negative Encounters As a Lesson

Negative experiences and people are a part of life, as are the ways that we let them affect us. When you are faced with negative experiences, look at them as a lesson. Imagine for a moment that you have a friend who betrayed your trust. Rather than seeing it as a negative experience, consider the friendship for what it was worth. Maybe the situation happened so that they betrayed your trust with this and not something even more serious.

Prepare for the Worst Case Scenario

Sometimes, regardless of how much we prepare, we find ourselves struggling to find the positivity and confidence to deal with a situation. Additionally, there are situations that we may have a negative outcome from, even with positive visualization. If you find yourself worrying about an obstacle that has arisen or at a loss for how to handle an issue, think about the worst thing that could happen. Often, people who chronically worry exaggerate the real dangers of a situation. Once you think about the worst thing that could happen, consider the likelihood of the even happening.

If you do find that it is likely the scenario could happen, consider what you could do in the situation. If there is nothing that you can do, then sit back and try to relax until you hear something new. It is not helpful to worry over situations that you have no control over.

Make a Plan to Tackle the Obstacle

When you are handling a real obstacle that you must deal with, the least stressful and most helpful thing that you can do to work toward your own success is make a plan to tackle the obstacle and get it out of your way.

Developing an End Goal

The first step of any plan is to know exactly what you intend to do. The reason for this is having a clear objective will keep you on track as you work toward the end goal. Consider exactly what the obstacle is that you are facing and what it would mean to overcome it. Then, write the obstacle down at the top of a piece of paper to keep you on track as you come up with a plan to tackle the obstacle.

Writing the Plan

Once you have an end goal, you can start breaking it down into steps. Each step of the plan should be manageable on its own and work toward the major goal of overcoming your obstacle. In addition to breaking down the steps, you may want to consider when each step should be done or write down specifics about how you intend to do each step (when steps are necessary).

Consciously Visualizing the Course of Action

After you have a clear-cut plan, you can begin visualization. Once again, you will go to a quiet environment and sit or lay comfortable. Close your eyes and focus on your breaths. Once you are relaxed, read over the individual steps of your plan, as well as your end goal. After you have read the steps, close your eyes once again. Visualize yourself completing each individual step and then envision the satisfaction that goes along with it. Feel the pride that accompanies you after completing each step and then the sense of happiness that will follow when you complete your entire goal.

Example Visualization for Overcoming Obstacles

For this visualization, imagine that you are at work one day and a new person starts. It turns out to be someone from high school that you do not get along with. You remember the incident and want to clear the air with your coworker but are shy. The pressure increases when your boss assigns you to work together.

The goal in this situation would be to address the misunderstanding between yourself and your classmate in the past, agree to leave the disagreement in the past, and work toward success at the office. To do this, you will need to come up with a plan of action to speak to your coworker.

Visualize yourself walking toward your coworker, with your shoulders back, your back straight, and your head held high. Feel the confidence that is oozing from you and filling the air.

As you approach your coworker, you think about what you want to say once again. You remind your coworker of this misunderstanding and assure him or her that you want to leave the past in the past. Then, you inform them that you have been assigned to work together recently and you would like to use that time to let bygones be bygones and work toward the success of the team. Seal your conversation with a friendly handshake and a plan to meet up in the future to discuss the project.

After visualizing the conversation, imagine yourself walking away. Feel the confidence and reassurance that now fills you, instead of the worry that was present earlier.

Chapter 6 – The Taking Action Visualization

Sometimes, the perfect companion to your visualization exercises is affirmations. Self-affirmations are short statements that give you the confidence and self-esteem that you need to start taking action in your life. After all, your visualizations will not be nearly as helpful if you do not have the follow through to go with them.

In this chapter, you will find 100 affirmations that will give you the confidence and the power necessary to start taking action in your life. Thee will have a much greater impact if you read them out loud or listen to them audibly:

Every action that I take moves me one step closer to

my goals…

Each action that I take toward my goal moves me closer

to success…

I strive to accelerate my progress toward my goals every day…

Each of my actions moves me toward bigger and better

successes…

Every one of my actions creates positive opportunities and

experiences

I act on each opportunity that is presented to me…

I am motivated toward my goals and my overall success…

Every one of my actions reflects the person that I dream of becoming…

I know what needs to be done and act on what needs to be done immediately…

Every step that I take will be in a positive direction forward toward my goals…

I am inspired each day to take actions toward my progress…

I see success as a journey and work to move on to bigger and

better things every day…

My actions and attitude are able to propel me toward

success…

All of my energy is directed toward positive actions…

I push myself to complete more difficult tasks first so that the

rest of the day flows easily…

My actions demonstrate my commitment toward progress

and success…

I invest my emotions, actions, and energies into producing

positive results…

I am in control of my successes by making positive changes

every day…

I look for new ways to pursue my goals every day…

My commitment to my goals can be seen through

my behaviors…

I honor each of my intentions by acting on them

every day…

I write down all of the actions I must take to strive

toward my goals…

My list of goals is ongoing and I strive toward it daily…

I feel a sense of invigoration with each positive action

that I take…

My visualizations make me feel empowered to succeed with

each of my goals…

I keep myself on track with moving toward my goals…

I know the first step in any goals is taking action…

I know that action is both required and necessary to

meet my goals…

I feel confident in my ability to change my own life

with visualization…

I know that changes must be made to strive for bigger and

better things…

I know that taking action is much more important than just

talking about goals…

I feel great satisfaction each time I cross something off of my

goals list…

I visualize myself being incredibly productive in working

toward my goals today…

I only put my energy toward actions that are empowering and

encouraging…

I work toward my dreams relentlessly…

I know that I can take charge of my life and work toward my dreams…

Every action that I take toward my goals is deliberate and intentional…

I talk and think less and take action toward my goals more…

Every positive action that I take throughout the day will bring me closer to my dreams…

The thoughts that I think and the actions that I take create the reality that I live in…

I use positive thoughts and positive actions to move me

toward my goals…

I find that the words I speak and the actions I take reflect

positive moves forward…

It brings me joy to see the progress I take toward my goals

each day…

I embrace success and refuse to believe any negative thoughts

that will hold me back…

I sever attachment from people and things holding me back

from my success…

I do have choices and I am free to create my own reality and

my highest level of success…

I let go of negative things and make more room for success to

come into my life…

I release the need to compare to others and realize that my

own success should reflect my needs…

I judge my own success by my own wants and desires and not

the wants and desires of others…

I will show the world what I can offer and fulfill my true

purpose…

I am here to leave a positive imprint on the world and will take

the actions to do so…

I release the negativity from my life so that I can focus

on positive actions…

I commit to being a positive influence on myself and the

world around me…

I am thankful for each day and the actions that I will take to

push myself toward success…

My options are not limited in any situations and I do have

the power to make choices…

My wants and desires deserve to be fulfilled because I deserve it…

Today holds infinite possibilities in the number of ways it can be a positive influence on my life…

I will interact with people that will help me on my path to greatness…

Instead of worrying about not having enough time, I will focus on using the time that I do have to work toward my goals…

My main focus will be serving my life's purpose and I will view anything that does not benefit me as a distraction…

I feel confident that once I commit to my dreams, they will start coming true…

I find it easy to direct my thoughts and actions so that they reflect my goals…

I will stay away from drama and negativity and surround myself with people and circumstances that bring positivity and success to my life…

I know that negative circumstances are a part of life and that I am confident to continue pursuing my dreams after a setback…

I choose to forgive others so that I can move forward with my life…

A wrong turn does not mean starting over, it just means following a new route…

I have the confidence and power to know that I can reach my goals…

I have great trust in my ability to make decisions to help me reach my goals…

I commit to doing at least one thing each day to progress toward my dreams…

I will view my journey of progress as what has already been accomplished, instead of focusing on what still needs to be completed…

My dreams and visions shape what I should accomplish, not

the desires of others…

I know that I am meant to do big things and refuse to let

anyone hold me back…

I choose to be who I want to be and accept others as who they

are and know that we are all on our own paths…

My approval of myself is more important than seeking

approval from others…

Some situations are out of my control and I refuse to worry

about what I cannot control…

I do not need anyone to make me successful, I am in charge of my own success…

The decisions I make affect my success and I do not need the approval of others…

I choose to be the best version of myself that I can be…

I refuse to let others affect me reaching my goals…

I will be mindful and aware as I go throughout the day…

I will be aware of the ways that my actions influence my

success throughout the day…

Fear will not get in the way of me striving for the things that I

want…

The path to happiness starts with me and I am ready to

commit to that change…

My visualizations will give me the courage to act in a way

that will push me to achieve my goals…

I know what I deserve from life and I take responsibility for

making it happen…

I refuse to give others the power to make me angry because I am responsible for the way I react and feel...

I am committed to my vision and use my visualizations to drive me forward...

Even the smallest of actions steps push me toward my goal...

Focusing my intentions and actions will bring me closer to my goal...

I will stay on my course, regardless of any obstacles I may face...

I know that some things happen to be a lesson and I can still

persevere after setbacks…

I will always let in clear opportunities…

I have a passion to find my purpose and this will drive me

toward my dreams…

I have endless talents and I will start using them today…

The qualities needed to reach my goals are inside of me…

I will abandon old habits that hold me back in place of new ones…

I will use visualization any time I find myself being discouraged…

I can handle any of the challenges that life may throw my way…

My visualizations will become my future…

Obstacles are moving out of my way and I am heading toward greatness…

You should read these affirmations out loud to yourself or listen to a recording of them. Once you have a clearer, more directed picture of your goals, you can write out your own affirmations to reflect on.

Conclusion

It is highly recommended that you continue to use visualization as you come across obstacles in life or as you find yourself reaching for new goals. You can change the visualizations that you use for any goal that you set - so continue to strive for bigger and better things once you have reached your current goals. There is no limit to the things that you can accomplish when you are able to visualize your success.

The next logical step here is to practice conscious visualization and start changing your life. Follow a regimen of practicing visualization for 15 minutes every morning before you start your day and every night before you go to bed. Use the steps provided in this book for your visualization. Follow this regimen for a period of at least 90 days and watch how it propels you forward and pushes you to succeed in every area of your life.

Best of luck as you push forward and change your life!

Jason.

References

Brouziyne, M., & Molinaro, C. (2005). Mental imagery combined with physical practice of approach shots for golf beginners. *Perceptual and motor skills.*, *101*(1), 203–11. Retrieved from http://www.ncbi.nlm.nih.gov/pubmed/16350625

Canfield, J. (2014, April 1). Visualize and affirm your desired outcomes: A step-by-step guide - America's leading authority on creating success and personal fulfillment. Retrieved September 25, 2016, from Success & Goal Achievement, http://jackcanfield.com/visualize-and-affirm-your-desired-outcomes-a-step-by-step-guide/

Hudson, P. (2016, June 15). The power of visualization in manifesting your success. Retrieved September 25, 2016, from Entrepreneurship, http://elitedaily.com/money/entrepreneurship/the-power-of-visualization-in-manifesting-your-success/

Mueller, S. (2016, August 2). The power of creative visualization. Retrieved September 25, 2016, from Mind, http://www.planetofsuccess.com/blog/2016/power-of-creative-visualization/

Niles, F. (2011, June 17). Why goal visualization works. *Huffington Post.* Retrieved from http://www.huffingtonpost.com/frank-niles-phd/visualization-goals_b_878424.html

Reyes, A. (2012, April 4). Alejandro Reyes. Retrieved September 25, 2016, from http://expertenough.com/1898/visualization-works

51585982R00119

Made in the USA
Middletown, DE
12 November 2017